MW00699996

RIVAL Crock·Pot ®

The Original and #1 Brand Slow Cooker

Incredibly Easy Recipes

Publications International, Ltd.

Favorite Brand Name Recipes at www.fbnr.com

Material on pages 4 and 5, and recipes on pages 42, 70, 96, 100, 102, and 108 © Sunbeam Products, Inc. All other material and recipes © Publications International, Ltd.

Rival®, the Rival Logo®, Crock-Pot®, the Crock-Pot Logo™, Smart Pot®, the Smart Pot® Logo, Versaware™, and the Versaware™ Logo are trademarks of Sunbeam Products, Inc.

Pictured on the front cover: Easy Beef Stew (page 82).

Pictured on the back cover: Asian Beef with Broccoli (page 88).

Photography on pages 7, 9, 11, 13, 15, 17, 19, 21, 23, 25, 29, 31, 33, 35, 37, 39, 41, 43, 47, 55, 57, 59, 61, 63, 65, 67, 69, 71, 73, 83, 85, 87, 89, 91, 93, 95, 97, 99, 101, 103, 105, 111, 113, 115, 117, 119, 121, 123, 133, 135, 137, 139, 143, 145, 147, 149, 151, and 153 by Stephen Hamilton Photographics, Inc., Chicago.

Photographers: Tate Hunt, Eric Coughlin
Photographers' assistant: Chris Gurley
Prop stylist: Tom Hamilton
Food stylists: Christianne Ingegno, Mary-Helen Steindler
Assistant food stylist: Lissa Levy

ISBN-13: 978-1-4127-2585-9
ISBN-10: 1-4127-2585-2

Manufactured in China.

8 7 6 5 4 3 2 1

Microwave cooking: Microwave ovens vary in wattage. Use the cooking times as guidelines and check for doneness before adding more time.

Preparation/cooking times: Preparation times are based on the approximate amount of time required to assemble the recipe before cooking, baking, chilling, or serving. These times include preparation steps such as measuring, chopping, and mixing. The fact that some preparation and cooking can be done simultaneously is taken into account. Preparation of optional ingredients and serving suggestions is not included.

CONTENTS

Slow Cooking
HINTS AND TIPS

How to get the best results from your Crock-Pot® slow cooker

Your **CROCK-POT®** slow cooker can be the best kitchen assistant you've ever had. Your family will enjoy delicious meals, while you save time and effort, thanks to the flavorful cooking process that works while you're away from home. To get the most from your **CROCK-POT®** slow cooker, just keep the following hints and tips in mind.

Stirring

Due to the nature of slow cooking, there's no need to stir the food unless the recipe method says to do so. In fact, taking the lid off to stir food causes your **CROCK-POT®** slow cooker to lose a significant amount of heat, which extends the cooking time. Therefore, it's best not to remove the lid.

Adding Ingredients at the End of Cooking Time

Certain ingredients are best added toward the end of the cooking time. These include:

- *Milk, sour cream, and yogurt:* Add during last 15 minutes.
- *Seafood and fish:* Add during last 30 to 60 minutes.
- *Fresh herbs:* Fresh herbs, such as basil, will turn black with long cooking, so if you want colorful fresh herbs, add those during the last 15 minutes of cooking time.

Pasta and Rice

For best results with rice, always use converted rice. Most recipes suggest adding pasta or rice halfway through the cooking time, for best texture. If the rice doesn't seem completely cooked after the suggested time, you may add an extra ½ cup to 1 cup of liquid per cup of rice and extend the cooking time by 30 to 60 minutes.

Herbs and Spices

When cooking with your **CROCK-POT**® slow cooker, use whole herbs and spices, rather than crushed or ground. The flavor and aroma of crushed or ground herbs may lessen during the extended cooking time. Be sure to taste the finished dish and add more seasonings if needed. If you prefer using colorful fresh herbs, add them during the last 15 minutes of cooking.

Cooking for Larger Quantity Yields

If you want to make a bigger batch in a larger unit, such as a 5-, 6-, or 7-quart **CROCK-POT**® slow cooker, the guidelines for doubling or tripling ingredients include:

• When preparing dishes with beef or pork in a larger unit, first browning the meat in a skillet yields the best results; the meat will cook more evenly.

• Roasted meats, chicken, and turkey quantities may be doubled or tripled, and seasonings adjusted by half. Caution: Flavorful spices such as garlic and chili powder will intensify during long slow cooking. Add just 25 to 50 percent more spices as needed to balance the flavors.

• When preparing a soup or a stew, you may double all ingredients except liquids, seasonings, and dried herbs. Initially, increase liquid volume by half, or as needed. The **CROCK-POT**® slow cooker lid collects steam, which condenses to keep foods moist and to maintain liquid volume. Do not double thickeners, such as cornstarch, at the beginning. You may always add more thickener later if it's necessary.

Cooking Temperatures and Food Safety

Cooking meats in your **CROCK-POT**® slow cooker is perfectly safe. According to the U.S. Department of Agriculture, bacteria in food is killed at a temperature of 165°F. Meats cooked in the **CROCK-POT**® slow cooker reach an internal temperature of 170°F in beef and as high as 190°F in poultry. It's important to follow the recommended cooking times and to keep the cover on your **CROCK-POT**® slow cooker during cooking to maintain food-safe temperatures.

One-Step

DISHES

COOKING CAN'T BE ANY SIMPLER; JUST ADD ALL THE INGREDIENTS, COOK AND SERVE!

Easy Beef Burgundy

MAKES 4 TO 6 SERVINGS

PREP TIME: 10 minutes
COOK TIME: LOW 6 to 8 hours

- 1½ pounds beef round steak or beef stew meat, cut into 1-inch pieces
- 1 can (10¾ ounces) condensed cream of mushroom soup, undiluted
- 1 cup red wine
- 1 small onion, chopped
- 1 can (4 ounces) sliced mushrooms, drained
- 1 package (1 ounce) dry onion soup mix
- 1 tablespoon minced garlic

Combine all ingredients in **CROCK-POT®** slow cooker. Cover; cook on LOW 6 to 8 hours or until beef is tender.

Parmesan Potato Wedges

MAKES 6 SERVINGS | *PREP TIME:* 15 minutes
COOK TIME: HIGH 4 hours

2 pounds red potatoes, cut into ½-inch wedges
¼ cup finely chopped yellow onion
1½ teaspoons dried oregano
½ teaspoon salt
¼ teaspoon black pepper, or to taste
2 tablespoons butter, cut into ⅛-inch pieces
¼ cup (1 ounce) grated Parmesan cheese

Layer potatoes, onion, oregano, salt, pepper and butter in
CROCK-POT® slow cooker. Cover; cook on HIGH 4 hours.
Transfer potatoes to serving platter and sprinkle with cheese.

Chicken Teriyaki

MAKES 4 SERVINGS | *PREP TIME:* 10 minutes
COOK TIME: LOW 2 hours

1 pound boneless skinless chicken tenders
1 can (6 ounces) pineapple juice
¼ cup soy sauce
1 tablespoon sugar
1 tablespoon minced fresh ginger
1 tablespoon minced garlic
1 tablespoon vegetable oil
1 tablespoon molasses
24 cherry tomatoes (optional)
2 cups hot cooked rice

Combine all ingredients, except rice, in **CROCK-POT®** slow
cooker. Cover; cook on LOW 2 hours or until chicken is
tender. Serve chicken and sauce over rice.

Parmesan Potato Wedges

Simple Slow Cooker Pork Roast

MAKES 6 SERVINGS

PREP TIME: 10 minutes
COOK TIME: LOW 6 to 8 hours

4 to 5 red potatoes, cut into bite-size pieces
4 carrots, cut into bite-size pieces
1 marinated pork loin roast* (3 to 4 pounds)
½ cup water
1 package (10 ounces) frozen baby peas
Salt and black pepper, to taste

*If marinated roast is unavailable, prepare marinade by mixing ¼ cup olive oil, 1 tablespoon minced garlic and 1½ tablespoons Italian seasoning. Place in large resealable plastic food storage bag with pork roast. Marinate in refrigerator at least 2 hours or overnight.

Place potatoes, carrots and pork roast in **CROCK-POT®** slow cooker. (If necessary, cut roast in half to fit.) Add water. Cover; cook on LOW 6 to 8 hours or until vegetables are tender. Add peas during last hour of cooking. Transfer pork to serving platter. Add salt and pepper, if desired. Slice and serve with vegetables.

Nice 'n Easy Italian Chicken

MAKES 4 SERVINGS

PREP TIME: 10 minutes
COOK TIME: LOW 6 to 8 hours

4 boneless skinless chicken breasts (about 1 pound)
8 ounces mushrooms, sliced
1 medium green bell pepper, chopped
1 medium zucchini, diced
1 medium onion, chopped
1 jar (26 ounces) pasta sauce
   Hot cooked linguini or spaghetti

Combine all ingredients, except pasta, in **CROCK-POT®** slow cooker. Cover; cook on LOW 6 to 8 hours or until chicken is tender. Serve over linguini.

Green Bean Casserole

MAKES 4 TO 6 SERVINGS

PREP TIME: 10 minutes
COOK TIME: LOW 3 to 4 hours

2 packages (10 ounces each) frozen green beans, thawed
1 can (10¾ ounces) condensed cream of mushroom soup, undiluted
1 tablespoon chopped parsley
1 tablespoon chopped roasted red peppers
1 teaspoon dried sage
½ teaspoon salt
½ teaspoon black pepper
¼ teaspoon ground nutmeg
½ cup toasted slivered almonds

Combine all ingredients, except almonds, in 2½-quart **CROCK-POT®** slow cooker. Cover; cook on LOW 3 to 4 hours. Sprinkle with almonds before serving.

Nice 'n Easy
Italian Chicken

Polska Kielbasa with Beer 'n Onions

MAKES 6 TO 8 SERVINGS

PREP TIME: 10 minutes
COOK TIME: LOW 4 to 5 hours

⅓ **cup honey mustard**
⅓ **cup packed dark brown sugar**
18 **ounces brown ale or beer**
2 **kielbasa sausages (16 ounces each), cut into 4-inch pieces**
2 **onions, quartered**

Combine honey mustard and brown sugar in **CROCK-POT®** slow cooker. Whisk in ale. Add sausage pieces. Top with onions. Cover; cook on LOW 4 to 5 hours, stirring occasionally.

Pumpkin-Cranberry Custard

MAKE 4 TO 6 SERVINGS

PREP TIME: 5 minutes
COOK TIME: HIGH 4 to 4½ hours

1 **can (30 ounces) pumpkin pie filling**
1 **can (12 ounces) evaporated milk**
1 **cup dried cranberries**
4 **eggs, beaten**
1 **cup crushed or whole gingersnap cookies (optional)**
Whipped cream (optional)

Combine pumpkin, evaporated milk, cranberries and eggs in **CROCK-POT®** slow cooker; mix thoroughly. Cover; cook on HIGH 4 to 4½ hours. Spoon into bowls. Serve with crushed or whole gingersnaps and whipped cream, if desired.

Polska Kielbasa
with Beer 'n Onions

Chicken and Wild Rice Casserole

MAKES 4 TO 6 SERVINGS

PREP TIME: 15 minutes
COOK TIME: LOW 3 to 4 hours

- 2 slices bacon, chopped
- 3 tablespoons olive oil
- 1½ pounds chicken thighs, trimmed of excess skin
- ½ cup diced onion
- ½ cup diced celery
- 2 tablespoons Worcestershire sauce
- ¾ teaspoon salt
- ¼ teaspoon black pepper
- ½ teaspoon dried sage
- 1 cup converted long-grain white rice
- 1 package (4 ounces) wild rice
- 6 ounces brown mushrooms,* wiped clean and quartered
- 3 cups hot chicken broth, or enough to cover chicken
- Salt and black pepper, to taste
- 2 tablespoons chopped parsley, for garnish

Use "baby bellas" or crimini mushrooms. Or, you may substitute white button mushrooms.

Microwave bacon on HIGH (100% power) 1 minute. Transfer to **CROCK-POT®** slow cooker. Add olive oil and spread evenly on bottom. Place chicken in **CROCK-POT®** slow cooker, skin side down. Add remaining ingredients in order given, except parsley. Cover; cook on LOW 3 to 4 hours, or until rice is tender. Uncover and let stand 15 minutes. Add salt and pepper, if desired. Remove skin before serving, if desired. Garnish with chopped parsley.

Chicken Mozambique

MAKES 4 SERVINGS

PREP TIME: 10 minutes
COOK TIME: LOW 8 hours
HIGH 6 hours

- 2½ pounds boneless skinless chicken breasts
- 1 cup white wine
- ½ cup (1 stick) butter, cut into small pieces
- 1 small onion, chopped
- 2 tablespoons minced garlic
- 2 tablespoons lemon juice
- 2 tablespoons hot pepper sauce
- 1 teaspoon salt
  Hot cooked rice
  Paprika, for garnish

Place all ingredients, except rice, in **CROCK-POT®** slow cooker. Cover; cook on LOW 8 hours or on HIGH 6 hours. Serve chicken and sauce over rice. Sprinkle with paprika, if desired.

Rough-Cut Smoky Red Pork

MAKES 8 SERVINGS

PREP TIME: 10 minutes
COOK TIME: HIGH 5 hours

1 pork shoulder roast (about 4 pounds)
1 can (14½ ounces) stewed tomatoes, well drained
1 can (6 ounces) tomato paste with basil, oregano and garlic
1 cup chopped red bell pepper
2 to 3 chipotle peppers in adobo sauce, finely chopped and mashed with fork*
1 teaspoon salt
1½ to 2 tablespoons sugar

For less heat, remove seeds from chipotle peppers before mashing

Coat 6-quart **CROCK-POT®** slow cooker with nonstick cooking spray. Place pork, fat side up, in bottom. Combine remaining ingredients, except sugar, in small bowl. Pour over pork. Cover; cook on HIGH 5 hours. Scrape tomato mixture into cooking liquid. Transfer pork to cutting board; let stand 15 minutes. Stir sugar into cooking liquid. Cook, uncovered, on HIGH 15 minutes longer. To serve, remove fat from pork and slice. Pour sauce over pork slices.

Hamburger Veggie Soup

MAKES 4 TO 6 SERVINGS

PREP TIME: 5 minutes
COOK TIME: HIGH 4 hours

1 pound 95% lean ground beef
1 bag (16 ounces) frozen mixed vegetables
1 package (10 ounces) frozen seasoning-blend vegetables
1 can (10¾ ounces) tomato soup, undiluted
1 can (14½ ounces) stewed tomatoes
2 cans (5½ ounces each) spicy vegetable juice
Salt and black pepper, to taste

Coat **CROCK-POT®** slow cooker with nonstick cooking spray. Crumble beef before placing in bottom. Add remaining ingredients. Stir well to blend. Cover; cook on HIGH 4 hours. If necessary, break up large pieces of beef. Add salt and pepper before serving, if desired.

Smothered Beef Patties

MAKES 8 SERVINGS

PREP TIME: 10 minutes
COOK TIME: LOW 8 hours

Worcestershire sauce, to taste
Garlic powder, to taste
Salt and black pepper, to taste
1 can (about 14 ounces) Mexican-style diced tomatoes with green chilies, undrained, divided
8 frozen beef patties, unthawed
1 onion, cut into 8 slices

Sprinkle bottom of **CROCK-POT®** slow cooker with small amount of Worcestershire sauce, garlic powder, salt, pepper and 2 tablespoons tomatoes. Add 1 frozen beef patty. Top with small amount of Worcestershire, garlic powder, salt, pepper, 2 tablespoons tomatoes and 1 onion slice. Repeat layers 7 times. Cover; cook on LOW 8 hours.

Hamburger
Veggie Soup

Mexican Cornbread Pudding

MAKES 8 SERVINGS | *PREP TIME:* 5 minutes
COOK TIME: LOW 2 to 2½ hours

1 can (14¾ ounces) cream-style corn
2 eggs
1 can (4 ounces) diced mild green chilies
2 tablespoons vegetable oil
¾ cup yellow cornmeal
2 tablespoons sugar
2 teaspoons baking powder
¾ teaspoon salt
½ cup shredded Cheddar cheese

Coat 2-quart **CROCK-POT®** slow cooker with nonstick cooking spray. Combine corn, eggs, chilies, oil, cornmeal, sugar, baking powder and salt in medium bowl. Stir well to blend. Pour into **CROCK-POT®** slow cooker. Cover; cook on LOW 2 to 2½ hours or until center is set. Sprinkle cheese over top. Cover and let stand 5 minutes or until cheese is melted.

Easy Beef Stroganoff

MAKES 4 TO 6 SERVINGS | *PREP TIME:* 5 minutes
COOK TIME: LOW 6 hours
HIGH 3 hours

3 cans (10¾ ounces each) condensed cream of
   mushroom soup, undiluted
1 cup sour cream
½ cup water
1 package (1 ounce) dry onion soup mix
2 pounds beef stew meat, cut into 1-inch pieces

Combine soup, sour cream, water and soup mix in **CROCK-POT®** slow cooker. Add beef; stir until well coated. Cover; cook on LOW 6 hours or on HIGH 3 hours.

Mexican Cornbread Pudding

Hungarian Lamb Goulash

MAKES 6 SERVINGS

PREP TIME: 10 minutes
COOK TIME: LOW 6 to 8 hours

1 package (16 ounces) frozen cut green beans
1 cup chopped onion
1¼ pounds lean lamb stew meat, cut into 1-inch pieces
1 can (15 ounces) chunky tomato sauce
1¾ cups fat-free reduced-sodium chicken broth
1 can (6 ounces) tomato paste
4 teaspoons paprika
3 cups hot cooked egg noodles

Place green beans and onion in **CROCK-POT®** slow cooker. Top with lamb. Combine remaining ingredients, except noodles, in large bowl; mix well. Pour over lamb. Cover; cook on LOW 6 to 8 hours. Stir gently before serving over noodles.

Creamy Chicken

MAKES 3 SERVINGS

PREP TIME: 5 minutes
COOK TIME: LOW 6 to 8 hours

3 boneless skinless chicken breasts *or* 6 boneless skinless chicken thighs
2 cans (10¾ ounces each) condensed cream of chicken soup, undiluted
1 can (14½ ounces) chicken broth
1 can (4 ounces) sliced mushrooms, drained
½ medium onion, diced
Salt and black pepper, to taste

Place all ingredients, except salt and pepper, in **CROCK-POT®** slow cooker. Cover; cook on LOW 6 to 8 hours. Add salt and pepper, if desired.

Hungarian Lamb Goulash

Meatless Sloppy Joes

MAKES 4 SERVINGS

PREP TIME: 15 minutes

COOK TIME: LOW 5 to 5½ hours

- 2 cups thinly sliced onions
- 2 cups chopped green bell peppers
- 1 can (about 15 ounces) kidney beans, drained and mashed
- 1 can (8 ounces) tomato sauce
- 2 tablespoons ketchup
- 1 tablespoon yellow mustard
- 2 cloves garlic, finely chopped
- 1 teaspoon chili powder

  Cider vinegar (optional)
- 4 sandwich rolls

Combine onions, bell peppers, beans, tomato sauce, ketchup, mustard, garlic and chili powder in **CROCK-POT®** slow cooker. Cover; cook on LOW 5 to 5½ hours or until vegetables are tender. Season to taste with cider vinegar, if desired. Serve on rolls.

4 INGREDIENTS

or Less

Chorizo Chili

MAKES 6 SERVINGS

PREP TIME: 5 minutes
COOK TIME: LOW 7 hours

- **1 pound 90% lean ground beef**
- **8 ounces bulk raw chorizo or ½ package (15 ounces) raw chorizo**
- **1 can (16 ounces) chili beans in chili sauce**
- **2 cans (14½ ounces) zesty chili-style diced tomatoes, undrained**

1. Place beef and chorizo in **CROCK-POT®** slow cooker. Break up with fork to form small chunks.

2. Stir in beans and tomatoes. Cover; cook on LOW 7 hours. Skim off and discard excess fat before serving.

Serving suggestion: *Top with sour cream or shredded cheese.*

Bacon and Onion Brisket

MAKES 6 SERVINGS

PREP TIME: 20 minutes
COOK TIME: HIGH 6 to 8 hours

6 slices bacon, cut crosswise into ½-inch strips

1 flat-cut boneless brisket, seasoned with salt and black pepper (about 2½ pounds)

3 medium onions, sliced

2 cans (10½ ounces each) condensed beef consommé, undiluted

1. Cook bacon strips in large skillet over medium-high heat about 3 minutes. Do not overcook. Transfer bacon with slotted spoon to 5-quart **CROCK-POT®** slow cooker.

2. Sear brisket in hot bacon fat on all sides, turning as it browns. Transfer to **CROCK-POT®** slow cooker.

3. Lower heat for skillet to medium. Add sliced onions to skillet. Cook and stir 3 to 5 minutes or until softened. Add to **CROCK-POT®** slow cooker. Pour in consommé. Cover; cook on HIGH 6 to 8 hours or until meat is tender.

4. Transfer brisket to cutting board and let rest 10 minutes. Slice brisket against the grain into thin slices, and arrange on platter. Add salt and pepper, if desired. Spoon bacon, onions, and cooking liquid over brisket to serve.

Easy Chocolate Pudding Cake

MAKES 16 SERVINGS

PREP TIME: 15 minutes
COOK TIME: HIGH 1½ hours

1 package (6-serving size) instant chocolate pudding and pie filling mix

3 cups milk

1 package (about 18 ounces) chocolate fudge cake mix, plus ingredients to prepare mix

Crushed peppermint candies (optional)

Whipped topping or ice cream (optional)

1. Coat **CROCK-POT®** slow cooker with nonstick cooking spray. Add pudding mix. Whisk in milk.

2. Prepare cake mix according to package directions. Carefully pour cake mix into **CROCK-POT®** slow cooker. *Do not stir.* Cover; cook on HIGH 1½ hours or until toothpick inserted into center comes out clean.

3. Spoon into cup or onto plate. Serve warm with crushed peppermint candies and whipped topping, if desired.

Slow Cooker Turkey Breast

MAKES 4 TO 6 SERVINGS

PREP TIME: 5 minutes
COOK TIME: LOW 6 to 8 hours
HIGH 2½ to 3 hours

½ to 1 teaspoon garlic powder, or to taste
½ to 1 teaspoon paprika, or to taste
1 turkey breast (4 to 6 pounds)
1 tablespoon dried parsley flakes, or to taste

1. Blend garlic powder and paprika. Rub into turkey skin. Place turkey in 6-quart **CROCK-POT®** slow cooker. Sprinkle on parsley. Cover; cook on LOW 6 to 8 hours or on HIGH 2½ to 3 hours or until internal temperature reaches 165°F when meat thermometer is inserted into thickest part of breast, not touching bone.

2. Transfer turkey to cutting board; cover with foil and let stand 10 to 15 minutes before carving. (Internal temperature will rise 5° to 10°F during stand time.)

Fantastic Pot Roast

MAKES 6 SERVINGS | *PREP TIME:* 5 minutes
COOK TIME: LOW 6 to 8 hours

1 can (12 ounces) cola
1 bottle (10 ounces) chili sauce
2 cloves garlic (optional)
2½ pounds boneless beef chuck roast

Combine cola, chili sauce and garlic, if desired, in
CROCK-POT® slow cooker. Add beef, and turn to coat.
Cover; cook on LOW 6 to 8 hours. Serve with sauce.

Chili and Cheese "Baked" Potato Supper

MAKES 4 SERVINGS | *PREP TIME:* 10 minutes
COOK TIME: LOW 8 to 10 hours
HIGH 4 to 5 hours

4 russet potatoes (8 ounces each)
2 cups prepared chili
½ cup (2 ounces) shredded Cheddar cheese
4 tablespoons sour cream (optional)
2 green onions, sliced

1. Prick potatoes in several places with fork. Wrap potatoes
in aluminum foil. Place in **CROCK-POT®** slow cooker. Cover;
cook on LOW 8 to 10 hours or on HIGH 4 to 5 hours. Carefully
unwrap potatoes and place on serving dish.

2. Heat chili in microwave or on stovetop. Split hot potatoes
and spoon chili on top. Sprinkle with cheese, sour cream, if
desired, and green onions.

Fantastic Pot Roast

Posole

MAKES 8 SERVINGS

PREP TIME: 15 minutes
COOK TIME: HIGH 5 hours plus
LOW 10 hours

3 pounds boneless pork, cubed
3 cans (14 ounces each) white hominy, drained
1 cup chili sauce

Combine all ingredients in **CROCK-POT®** slow cooker. Cover; cook on HIGH 5 hours. Reduce temperature to LOW. Cook on LOW 10 hours longer.

Easy Family Burritos

MAKES 8 SERVINGS

PREP TIME: 5 minutes
COOK TIME: LOW 9 to 11 hours

1 boneless beef chuck shoulder roast (2 to 3 pounds)
1 jar (24 ounces) *or* 2 jars (16 ounces each) salsa
Flour tortillas, warmed
Optional toppings: shredded cheese, sour cream, salsa, shredded lettuce, diced tomato, diced onion or guacamole

1. Place roast in **CROCK-POT®** slow cooker; top with salsa. Cover; cook on LOW 8 to 10 hours.

2. Remove beef from **CROCK-POT®** slow cooker. Shred beef with 2 forks. Return to cooking liquid and mix well. Cover; cook 1 to 2 hours longer or until heated through.

3. Serve shredded beef wrapped in warm tortillas. Top as desired.

Posole

Cherry Delight

MAKES 8 TO 10 SERVINGS

PREP TIME: 10 minutes
COOK TIME: LOW 3 to 4 hours
HIGH 1½ to 2 hours

1 can (21 ounces) cherry pie filling
1 package (18¼ ounces) yellow cake mix
½ cup (1 stick) butter, melted
⅓ cup chopped walnuts
Whipped topping or vanilla ice cream (optional)

1. Place pie filling in **CROCK-POT®** slow cooker.

2. Mix together cake mix and butter in medium bowl. Spread evenly over cherry filling. Sprinkle walnuts on top. Cover; cook on LOW 3 to 4 hours or HIGH 1½ to 2 hours.

3. Spoon into serving dishes, and serve warm with whipped topping or ice cream, if desired.

BBQ Roast Beef Sandwiches

MAKES 10 TO 12 SANDWICHES

PREP TIME: 5 minutes
COOK TIME: LOW 2 hours

2 pounds boneless cooked roast beef*
1 bottle (12 ounces) barbecue sauce
1½ cups water
10 to 12 sandwich rolls, halved

Use 2 pounds deli roast beef. You may substitute a 3- to 4-pound beef chuck shoulder roast; do not add water, and cook on LOW 8 to 10 hours.

1. Combine beef, barbecue sauce and water in **CROCK-POT®** slow cooker. Cover; cook on LOW 2 hours.

2. Remove beef from **CROCK-POT®** slow cooker. Shred beef with 2 forks. Return to **CROCK-POT®** slow cooker and mix well. Serve on rolls.

Glazed Pork Loin

MAKES 4 SERVINGS

PREP TIME: 5 minutes
COOK TIME: LOW 8 hours
HIGH 4 hours

1 bag (1 pound) baby carrots
4 boneless pork loin chops
1 jar (8 ounces) apricot preserves

Place carrots on bottom of **CROCK-POT®** slow cooker. Place pork on carrots; spread with preserves. Cover; cook on LOW 8 hours or on HIGH 4 hours.

BBQ Roast Beef Sandwiches

Autumn Delight

MAKES 4 TO 6 SERVINGS | *PREP TIME:* 15 minutes
COOK TIME: LOW 4 to 6 hours

1 tablespoon olive oil
4 to 6 beef cubed steaks
2 cans (10¾ ounces each) condensed cream of
    mushroom soup, undiluted
1 cup water
1 package (1 ounce) dry onion soup mix *or*
    mushroom soup mix

1. Heat oil in large skillet over medium heat until hot. Lightly brown steaks on both sides. Transfer to **CROCK-POT®** slow cooker.

2. Combine soup, water and dry soup mix in large bowl; mix well. Pour over steaks. Cover; cook on LOW 4 to 6 hours.

Harvest Ham Supper

MAKES 6 SERVINGS | *PREP TIME:* 10 minutes
COOK TIME: LOW 6 to 8 hours

6 carrots, cut into 2-inch pieces
3 medium sweet potatoes, quartered
1 to 1½ pounds boneless ham
1 cup maple syrup

1. Arrange carrots and potatoes in bottom of **CROCK-POT®** slow cooker to form rack.

2. Place ham on top of vegetables. Pour syrup over ham and vegetables. Cover; cook on LOW 6 to 8 hours.

Autumn Delight

Easy Cheesy BBQ Chicken

MAKES 6 SERVINGS

PREP TIME: 15 minutes
COOK TIME: LOW 8 to 9 hours

6 boneless skinless chicken breasts (about 1½ pounds)

1 bottle (26 ounces) barbecue sauce

6 slices bacon

6 slices Swiss cheese

1. Place chicken in **CROCK-POT®** slow cooker. Cover with barbecue sauce. Cover; cook on LOW 8 to 9 hours. (If sauce becomes too thick during cooking, add a little water.)

2. Before serving, cut bacon slices in half. Cook bacon in microwave or on stove top, keeping bacon flat. Place 2 pieces cooked bacon on each chicken breast in **CROCK-POT®** slow cooker. Top with cheese. Cover; cook on HIGH until cheese melts.

Spicy Shredded Chicken

MAKES 6 SERVINGS

PREP TIME: 5 minutes
COOK TIME: LOW 6 to 8 hours

**6 boneless skinless chicken breasts
(about 1½ pounds)
1 jar (16 ounces) salsa
Flour tortillas, warmed
Optional toppings: shredded cheese, sour cream,
shredded lettuce, diced tomato, diced onion or
sliced avocado**

1. Place chicken in **CROCK-POT®** slow cooker. Cover with salsa. Cover; cook on LOW 6 to 8 hours or until chicken is tender and no longer pink in center.

2. Shred chicken with 2 forks. Serve with warmed tortillas and top as desired.

Cheesy Slow Cooker Potatoes

MAKES 6 SERVINGS

PREP TIME: 5 minutes
COOK TIME: LOW 6 to 8 hours

**1 bag (32 ounces) shredded hash browns
2 cans (10¾ ounces each) condensed Cheddar
cheese soup, undiluted
1 can (12 ounces) evaporated milk
1 cup chopped onion**

Combine all ingredients in **CROCK-POT®** slow cooker. Cover; cook on LOW 6 to 8 hours.

Spicy Shredded Chicken

Italian Beef

MAKES 8 SERVINGS | *PREP TIME:* 5 minutes
COOK TIME: LOW 10 hours

1 beef rump roast (3 to 5 pounds)
1 can (14 ounces) beef broth
2 cups mild giardiniera
8 crusty Italian bread rolls, split

1. Place roast in 5-quart **CROCK-POT®** slow cooker; add broth and giardiniera. Cover; cook on LOW 10 hours.

2. Remove beef from **CROCK-POT®** slow cooker. Shred beef with 2 forks. Return to cooking liquid; mix well. To serve, spoon beef and sauce onto rolls.

Orange Chicken

MAKES 4 SERVINGS | *PREP TIME:* 5 minutes
COOK TIME: LOW 5 to 6 hours

1 can (12 ounces) orange soda
½ cup soy sauce
4 boneless skinless chicken breasts (about 1 pound)
Hot cooked rice

Pour soda and soy sauce into **CROCK-POT®** slow cooker. Add chicken and turn to coat. Cover; cook on LOW 5 to 6 hours. Serve over rice.

Italian Beef

Family
FAVORITES

EASY-TO-MAKE DISHES THAT WILL PLEASE THE MOST PICKY PALATES

Pizza Soup

MAKES 4 SERVINGS

PREP TIME: 10 minutes
COOK TIME: LOW 6 to 7 hours

2 cans (14½ ounces each) stewed tomatoes with
　　Italian seasonings, undrained
2 cups beef broth
1 cup sliced mushrooms
1 small onion, chopped
1 tablespoon tomato paste
¼ teaspoon salt, or to taste
¼ teaspoon black pepper, or to taste
½ pound hot turkey Italian sausage, casings removed
　　Shredded mozzarella cheese

1. Combine tomatoes with juice, broth, mushrooms, onion, tomato paste, salt and pepper in 4- or 5-quart **CROCK-POT®** slow cooker.

2. Shape sausage into marble-size balls. Gently stir into soup mixture. Cover; cook on LOW 6 to 7 hours. Adjust salt and pepper, if necessary. Serve with cheese.

Pork Chops with Dried Fruit and Onions

MAKES 6 SERVINGS

PREP TIME: 20 minutes
COOK TIME: LOW 3½ to 4 hours

6 **bone-in end-cut pork chops (about 2½ pounds)**
Salt and black pepper, to taste
3 **tablespoons vegetable oil**
2 **onions, diced**
2 **cloves garlic, minced**
¼ **teaspoon dried sage**
¾ **cup quartered pitted dried plums**
¾ **cup orchard mix or mixed dried fruit, chopped**
3 **cups unsweetened unfiltered apple juice**
1 **bay leaf**

1. Season pork chops with salt and pepper. Heat oil in large skillet over medium-high heat until hot. Sear pork on both sides to brown, cooking in batches, if necessary. Transfer to 5-quart **CROCK-POT®** slow cooker.

2. Add onions to hot skillet. Cook and stir over medium heat until softened. Add garlic and cook 30 seconds more. Sprinkle sage over mixture. Add dried plums, mixed fruit and apple juice. Bring mixture to a boil. Reduce heat and simmer, uncovered, 3 minutes, scraping bottom and sides of pan to release browned bits. Ladle mixture over pork chops.

3. Add bay leaf. Cover; cook on LOW 3½ to 4 hours, or until pork chops are tender. Remove bay leaf. Add salt and pepper, if desired. To serve, spoon fruit and cooking liquid over pork chops.

Open-Face Provençal Vegetable Sandwich

MAKES 6 SERVINGS

PREP TIME: 15 minutes
COOK TIME: LOW 5 to 6 hours

- 2 cups sliced shiitake mushroom caps
- 1 large zucchini, halved lengthwise and sliced ¼ inch thick
- 1 large red bell pepper, cored, quartered lengthwise and thinly sliced
- 1 small onion, sliced lengthwise ¼ inch thick
- 1 small jalapeño pepper,* cored, seeded and minced
- ¼ cup vegetable or chicken broth
- ¼ cup pitted kalamata olives
- 2 tablespoons capers
- 1 garlic clove, minced
- 1½ tablespoons olive oil, divided
- ½ teaspoon crushed dried oregano
- ¼ teaspoon salt, or to taste
- ¼ teaspoon black pepper, or to taste
- 4 teaspoons white wine vinegar
- Crusty bread, cut into thick slices
- Shredded mozzarella cheese (optional)

Jalapeño peppers can sting and irritate the skin, so wear rubber gloves when handling peppers and do not touch eyes.

1. Combine mushrooms, zucchini, bell pepper, onion, jalapeño, broth, olives, capers, garlic, 1 tablespoon olive oil, oregano, salt and black pepper in 5-quart **CROCK-POT®** slow cooker. Cover; cook on LOW 5 to 6 hours.

2. Turn off **CROCK-POT®** slow cooker. Stir in vinegar and remaining ½ tablespoon oil. Let stand, uncovered, 15 to

30 minutes until vegetables absorb some of liquid. (Vegetable mixture should be lukewarm.) Add salt and pepper, if desired.

3. To serve, spoon onto bread. If desired, sprinkle each serving with 2 to 3 tablespoons shredded mozzarella cheese and broil 30 seconds, or until cheese melts and browns.

Note: *You can substitute goat cheese or feta cheese; it's not necessary to broil these cheeses. Also, vegetables can be served as a side dish, if desired.*

Chicken in Enchilada Sauce

MAKES 4 SERVINGS | *PREP TIME:* 10 minutes
COOK TIME: LOW 6 to 7 hours

1 can (14½ ounces) diced tomatoes with smoked chipotle chiles,* undrained
1 can (10 ounces) enchilada sauce
1 cup frozen or canned corn
¼ teaspoon ground cumin
¼ teaspoon black pepper, or to taste
1½ pounds boneless skinless chicken thighs, cut into bite-size pieces
2 tablespoons minced cilantro
½ cup shredded pepper jack cheese**
Sliced green onions, for garnish

If tomatoes with smoked chipotle chiles aren't available, use diced tomatoes with chiles or plain diced tomatoes plus ¼ teaspoon crushed red pepper flakes.

**For a less spicy dish, use Monterey Jack cheese.*

1. Combine tomatoes with juice, enchilada sauce, corn, cumin, and pepper in **CROCK-POT®** slow cooker. Add chicken; mix well to combine. Cover; cook on LOW 6 to 7 hours.

2. Stir in cilantro. Spoon chicken and sauce into 4 shallow bowls. Sprinkle each serving with 2 tablespoons cheese. Garnish with green onions, if desired.

Southwestern Salmon Po' Boys

MAKES 4 SERVINGS | **PREP TIME:** 10 minutes
COOK TIME: HIGH 1½ hours

1 red bell pepper, cored, seeded and sliced
1 green bell pepper, cored, seeded and sliced
1 onion, sliced
½ teaspoon zesty Southwest chipotle seasoning
¼ teaspoon salt
¼ teaspoon black pepper
4 salmon fillets (about 6 ounces each),
   rinsed and patted dry
¾ cup Italian dressing
¼ cup water
4 large French sandwich rolls, split or French bread
   cut into 6-inch pieces and split
Chipotle mayonnaise,* to taste
Fresh cilantro, for garnish
½ lemon, cut into 4 wedges

If unavailable, combine ¼ cup mayonnaise with ½ teaspoon adobo sauce. Or, substitute regular mayonnaise.

1. Coat 5- or 6-quart **CROCK-POT®** slow cooker with nonstick cooking spray. Arrange half of sliced bell peppers and onions in bottom.

2. Blend seasoning, salt and black pepper. Season both sides of salmon. Place salmon on top of vegetables in **CROCK-POT®** slow cooker. Pour Italian dressing over salmon. Spread remaining peppers and onions over salmon. Add water. Cover; cook on HIGH 1½ hours.

3. Toast rolls, if desired. Spread lids with chipotle mayonnaise and garnish with cilantro. Spoon 1 to 2 tablespoons cooking liquid onto roll bottoms. Place warm fillet on each roll (remove skin first, if desired). Top with vegetable mixture and roll lids. Serve with lemon wedge.

Chicken and
Spicy Black Bean Tacos

MAKES 4 SERVINGS | *PREP TIME:* 10 minutes
COOK TIME: HIGH 1¾ hours

1 can (15 ounces) black beans, rinsed and drained
1 can (10 ounces) tomatoes with mild green chilies, drained
1½ teaspoons chili powder
¾ teaspoon ground cumin
1 tablespoon plus 1 teaspoon extra-virgin olive oil, divided
12 ounces boneless skinless chicken breasts, rinsed and patted dry
12 crisp corn taco shells
Optional toppings: shredded lettuce, diced tomatoes, shredded cheese, sour cream, ripe olives

1. Coat **CROCK-POT®** slow cooker with nonstick cooking spray. Add beans and tomatoes with chilies. Blend chili powder and cumin with 1 teaspoon oil and rub onto chicken breasts. Place chicken in **CROCK-POT®** slow cooker. Cover; cook on HIGH 1¾ hours.

2. Remove chicken and slice. Transfer bean mixture to bowl using slotted spoon. Stir in 1 tablespoon oil.

3. To serve, warm taco shells according to package directions. Fill with equal amounts of bean mixture and chicken. Top as desired.

Hearty Chicken Chili

MAKES 6 SERVINGS

PREP TIME: 15 minutes
COOK TIME: LOW 7 hours

1 medium onion, finely chopped
1 small jalapeño pepper,* cored, seeded and minced
1 small garlic clove, minced
1½ teaspoons medium-hot chili powder
¾ teaspoon salt, or to taste
½ teaspoon black pepper, or to taste
½ teaspoon ground cumin
½ teaspoon crushed dried oregano
2 cans (15½ ounces) hominy, drained and rinsed
1 can (15 ounces) pinto beans, drained and rinsed
1½ pounds boneless skinless chicken thighs, cut into 1-inch pieces
1 cup chicken broth
1 tablespoon all-purpose flour (optional)
Chopped parsley or cilantro, for garnish

Jalapeño peppers can sting and irritate the skin, so wear rubber gloves when handling peppers and do not touch eyes. For a hotter dish, add ¼ teaspoon crushed red pepper flakes with the seasonings.

1. Combine onion, jalapeño, garlic, chili powder, salt, pepper, cumin, and oregano in **CROCK-POT®** slow cooker.

2. Add hominy, beans, chicken and broth. Stir well to combine. Cover; cook on LOW 7 hours.

3. If thicker gravy is desired, combine 1 tablespoon flour and 3 tablespoons cooking liquid in small bowl. Add to **CROCK-POT®** slow cooker. Cover; cook on HIGH 10 minutes, or until thickened. Serve in bowls and garnish as desired.

Cuban Pork Sandwiches

MAKES 8 SERVINGS

PREP TIME: 20 minutes
COOK TIME: LOW 7 to 8 hours
HIGH 3½ to 4 hours

1 pork loin roast (about 2 pounds)
½ cup orange juice
2 tablespoons lime juice
1 tablespoon minced garlic
1½ teaspoons salt
½ teaspoon crushed red pepper flakes
8 crusty bread rolls, split in half (6 inches each)
2 tablespoons yellow mustard
8 slices Swiss cheese
8 thin ham slices
4 small dill pickles, thinly sliced lengthwise

1. Coat **CROCK-POT®** slow cooker with nonstick cooking spray. Add pork loin.

2. Combine orange juice, lime juice, garlic, salt and pepper flakes in small bowl. Pour over pork. Cover; cook on LOW 7 to 8 hours or on HIGH 3½ to 4 hours. Transfer pork to cutting board and allow to cool. Cut into thin slices.

3. To serve, spread mustard on both sides of rolls. Divide pork slices among roll bottoms. Top with Swiss cheese slice, ham slice and pickle slices. Cover with top of roll.

4. Coat large skillet with nonstick cooking spray and heat over medium heat until hot. Working in batches, arrange sandwiches in skillet. Cover with foil and top with dinner plate to press down sandwiches. (If necessary, weight with 2 to 3 cans to compress sandwiches lightly.) Heat until cheese is slightly melted, about 8 minutes.* Serve immediately.

*Or use tabletop grill to compress and heat sandwiches.

Mock Piggies

MAKES 4 SERVINGS | *PREP TIME:* 20 minutes
COOK TIME: LOW 8 hours

1 head cabbage
1 pound 90% lean ground beef
1 cup cooked rice
1 onion, chopped
1 teaspoon salt
½ teaspoon black pepper
2 cans (10¾ ounces each) tomato soup
1 can water (measured in soup can)

1. Heat large saucepan of water to boiling point. Cut out core of cabbage. Place cabbage head into boiling water. Cook until leaves separate and are tender.

2. Meanwhile, place ground beef, rice, onion, salt and pepper in large bowl. Stir well to combine.

3. Line bottom of **CROCK-POT®** slow cooker with half of cabbage leaves. Place meat mixture on top.

4. Combine soup and water. Pour half of soup mixture over meat. Arrange remaining cabbage over meat to cover completely. Top with remaining soup. Cover; cook on LOW 8 hours.

Greek Chicken Pitas with Creamy Mustard Sauce

MAKES 4 SERVINGS | *PREP TIME:* 10 minutes
COOK TIME: HIGH 1¾ hours

FILLING

- 1 medium green bell pepper, cored, seeded and sliced into ½-inch strips
- 1 medium onion, cut into 8 wedges
- 1 pound boneless skinless chicken breasts, rinsed and patted dry
- 1 tablespoon extra-virgin olive oil
- 2 teaspoons dried Greek seasoning blend
- ¼ teaspoon salt

SAUCE

- ¼ cup plain fat-free yogurt
- ¼ cup mayonnaise
- 1 tablespoon prepared mustard
- ¼ teaspoon salt

- 4 whole pita rounds
- ½ cup crumbled feta cheese
- Optional toppings: sliced cucumbers, sliced tomatoes, kalamata olives

1. Coat **CROCK-POT®** slow cooker with nonstick cooking spray. Place bell pepper and onion in bottom. Add chicken, and drizzle on oil. Sprinkle evenly with seasoning and ¼ teaspoon salt. Cover; cook on HIGH 1¾ hours or until chicken is no longer pink in center (vegetables will be slightly tender-crisp).

2. Remove chicken and slice. Remove vegetables using slotted spoon.

3. Prepare sauce: Combine yogurt, mayonnaise, mustard and ¼ teaspoon salt in small bowl. Whisk until smooth.

4. Warm pitas according to package directions. Cut in half, and layer with chicken, sauce, vegetables and feta cheese. Top as desired.

Spanish Chicken with Rice

MAKES 6 SERVINGS

PREP TIME: 20 minutes
COOK TIME: HIGH 3½ to 4 hours

2 tablespoons olive oil

11 ounces cooked linguiça or kielbasa, sliced into ½-inch rounds

6 boneless skinless chicken thighs (about 1 pound)

1 onion, diced

5 garlic cloves, minced

2 cups converted long-grain white rice

½ cup diced carrots

1 red bell pepper, cored, seeded and diced

½ teaspoon salt

¼ teaspoon black pepper

¼ teaspoon saffron threads (optional)

3½ cups hot chicken broth

½ cup frozen peas, thawed

1. Heat oil in medium skillet over medium heat until hot. Add sausage and brown on both sides. Transfer to **CROCK-POT®** slow cooker with slotted spoon.

2. Add chicken to skillet and brown on all sides. Transfer to **CROCK-POT®** slow cooker. Add onions to skillet, and cook and stir until soft. Stir in garlic and cook 30 seconds longer. Transfer to **CROCK-POT®** slow cooker.

3. Add rice, carrots, bell pepper, salt, black pepper and saffron, if desired. Pour broth over mixture. Cover; cook on HIGH 3½ to 4 hours.

4. Before serving, stir in peas. Cook 15 minutes or until heated through.

Country Chicken and Vegetables with Creamy Herb Sauce

MAKES 4 SERVINGS

PREP TIME: 20 minutes
COOK TIME: HIGH 3½ hours

1 pound new potatoes, cut into ½-inch wedges
1 medium onion, cut into 8 wedges
½ cup coarsely chopped celery
4 bone-in chicken drumsticks, skinned
4 bone-in chicken thighs, skinned
1 can (10¾ ounces) cream of chicken soup
1 packet (1 ounce) ranch-style dressing mix
½ teaspoon dried thyme
¼ teaspoon black pepper, or to taste
½ cup heavy cream
  Salt, to taste
¼ cup finely chopped green onions (green and
    white parts)

1. Coat **CROCK-POT®** slow cooker with nonstick cooking spray. Arrange potatoes, onion and celery in bottom. Add chicken. Combine soup, dressing mix, thyme and pepper in small bowl. Spoon mixture evenly over chicken and vegetables. Cover; cook on HIGH 3½ hours.

2. Transfer chicken to shallow serving bowl with slotted spoon. Add cream and salt, if desired, to cooking liquid. Stir well to blend. Pour sauce over chicken. Garnish with green onions.

Note: *To skin chicken easily, grasp skin with paper towel and pull away. Repeat with fresh paper towel for each piece of chicken, discarding skins and towels.*

Best Beef Brisket Sandwich Ever

MAKES 10 TO 12 SERVINGS

PREP TIME: 10 minutes
COOK TIME: LOW 10 hours

- 2 cups apple cider, divided
- 1 head garlic, cloves separated, crushed and peeled
- 2 tablespoons whole peppercorns
- 1/3 cup chopped fresh thyme *or* 2 tablespoons dried thyme
- 1 tablespoon mustard seeds
- 1 tablespoon Cajun seasoning
- 1 teaspoon ground allspice
- 1 teaspoon ground cumin
- 1 teaspoon celery seeds
- 2 to 4 whole cloves
- 1 beef brisket (about 3 pounds)
- 1 bottle (12 ounces) dark beer
- 10 to 12 sourdough sandwich rolls, sliced in half

1. Combine ½ cup cider, garlic, peppercorns, thyme, mustard seeds, Cajun seasoning, allspice, cumin, celery seeds and cloves in large resealable plastic food storage bag. Add brisket. Seal bag; marinate in refrigerator overnight.

2. Place brisket and marinade in **CROCK-POT®** slow cooker. Add remaining 1½ cups apple cider and beer. Cover; cook on LOW 10 hours or until brisket is tender.

3. Strain sauce; drizzle over meat. Slice brisket and place on sandwich rolls.

Honey Ribs

MAKES 4 SERVINGS

PREP TIME: 10 to 20 minutes
COOK TIME: LOW 6 to 8 hours
HIGH 4 to 6 hours

1 can (10¾ ounces) condensed beef consommé, undiluted

½ cup water

3 tablespoons soy sauce

2 tablespoons honey

2 tablespoons maple syrup

2 tablespoons barbecue sauce

½ teaspoon dry mustard

2 pounds pork baby back ribs, trimmed

1. Combine consommé, water, soy sauce, honey, maple syrup, barbecue sauce and mustard in **CROCK-POT®** slow cooker; mix well.

2. Cut ribs into 3- to 4-rib portions. Transfer to **CROCK-POT®** slow cooker. (If ribs are especially fatty, broil 10 minutes before adding.) Cover; cook on LOW 6 to 8 hours or on HIGH 4 to 6 hours or until ribs are tender.

3. Cut into individual ribs. Serve with sauce.

Backroads Ham and Potato Casserole

MAKES 4 TO 6 SERVINGS

PREP TIME: 15 minutes
COOK TIME: HIGH 3 to 5 hours

- 2 pounds baking potatoes, cut into 1-inch cubes
- ½ teaspoon dried thyme
- 12 ounces cubed ham
- 1 can (10¾ ounces) cream of chicken soup
- 4 ounces cream cheese, cut into ½-inch cubes
- ½ cup finely chopped green onion
- ½ cup frozen green peas, thawed

1. Coat **CROCK-POT®** slow cooker with nonstick cooking spray. Place potatoes in bottom. Add thyme and ham. Spread soup evenly over potatoes and ham. Cover; cook on HIGH 3 to 5 hours.

2. Gently stir in cream cheese, green onion and peas. Cover; cook 5 minutes longer or until cheese is melted.

Ham and Cheese Pasta Bake

MAKES 6 SERVINGS

PREP TIME: 15 minutes
COOK TIME: LOW 3½ to 4 hours

- **6 cups water**
- **2 teaspoons salt**
- **12 ounces rigatoni**
- **1 ham steak, cubed**
- **1 container (10 ounces) refrigerated light Alfredo sauce**
- **2 cups mozzarella cheese, divided**
- **2 cups hot half-and-half**
- **1 tablespoon cornstarch**

1. Bring water to a boil in medium saucepan. Stir in salt. Add rigatoni and boil 7 minutes. Drain well and transfer to **CROCK-POT®** slow cooker.

2. Stir in ham, Alfredo sauce and 1 cup cheese. Whisk together half-and-half and cornstarch. Pour half-and-half mixture over pasta to cover. Sprinkle on remaining cheese. Cover; cook on LOW 3½ to 4 hours. (Dish is done when rigatoni is tender and liquid is absorbed.)

Comforting
CLASSICS

HAVE EVERYONE'S FAVORITE MEAL
READY FOR SIT-DOWN SUPPERS

Easy Beef Stew

MAKES 6 TO 8 SERVINGS

PREP TIME: 15 minutes
COOK TIME: LOW 8 to 10 hours

1½ to 2 pounds beef stew meat, cut into 1-inch cubes
4 medium potatoes, cut into 1-inch cubes
4 carrots, cut into 1½-inch pieces *or*
    4 cups baby carrots
1 medium onion, cut into 8 wedges
2 cans (8 ounces each) tomato sauce
1 teaspoon salt
½ teaspoon black pepper
    Chopped parsley, for garnish

Combine all ingredients in **CROCK-POT®** slow cooker. Cover; cook on LOW 8 to 10 hours or until vegetables are tender. Garnish as desired.

Zesty Chicken and Rice Supper

MAKES 3 TO 4 SERVINGS

PREP TIME: 10 minutes
COOK TIME: LOW 6 to 8 hours
HIGH 3 to 4 hours

**2 boneless skinless chicken breasts,
    cut into 1-inch pieces**
2 large bell peppers, coarsely chopped
1 small onion, chopped
1 can (28 ounces) diced tomatoes, undrained
1 cup uncooked converted long-grain white rice
1 cup water
1 package (about 1 ounce) taco seasoning
1 teaspoon salt
1 teaspoon black pepper
1 teaspoon ground red pepper
Shredded Cheddar cheese (optional)

Place all ingredients, except cheese, in **CROCK-POT®** slow cooker. Stir well to combine. Cover; cook on LOW 6 to 8 hours or on HIGH 3 to 4 hours. Garnish with cheese, if desired.

Sweet and Sour Chicken

MAKE 4 SERVINGS

PREP TIME: 10 minutes
COOK TIME: LOW 2½ to 3½ hours

- ¼ **cup chicken broth**
- 2 **tablespoons low-sodium soy sauce**
- 2 **tablespoons hoisin sauce**
- 1 **tablespoon cider vinegar**
- 1 **tablespoon tomato paste**
- 2 **teaspoons packed brown sugar**
- 1 **garlic clove, minced**
- ¼ **teaspoon black pepper**
- 1 **pound boneless skinless chicken thighs, cut into 1-inch pieces**
- 2 **teaspoons cornstarch**
- 2 **tablespoons minced chives**
- **Hot cooked rice**

1. Combine broth, soy sauce, hoisin sauce, vinegar, tomato paste, brown sugar, garlic and pepper in **CROCK-POT®** slow cooker. Stir well to mix.

2. Add chicken thighs, and stir well to coat. Cover; cook on LOW 2½ to 3½ hours.

3. Remove chicken with slotted spoon, and keep warm. Combine cornstarch and 2 tablespoons cooking liquid in small bowl. Add to **CROCK-POT®** slow cooker. Stir in chives. Turn heat to HIGH. Stir 2 minutes or until sauce is slightly thickened. Serve chicken and sauce over rice.

Asian Beef with Broccoli

MAKES 4 TO 6 SERVINGS

PREP TIME: 15 minutes
COOK TIME: HIGH 3 hours

1½ **pounds boneless chuck steak,
about 1½ inches thick, sliced into thin strips***
1 **can (10½ ounces) condensed beef consommé,
undiluted**
½ **cup oyster sauce**
2 **tablespoons cornstarch**
1 **bag (16 ounces) fresh broccoli florets**
Hot cooked rice
Sesame seeds, for garnish

*To make slicing steak easier, place in freezer for 30 minutes to firm up.

1. Place beef in 6-quart **CROCK-POT®** slow cooker. Pour consommé and oyster sauce over beef. Cover; cook on HIGH 3 hours.

2. Combine cornstarch and 2 tablespoons cooking liquid in small bowl. Add to **CROCK-POT®** slow cooker. Stir well to combine. Cover; cook 15 minutes longer or until thickened.

3. Poke holes in broccoli bag with fork. Microwave on HIGH (100% power) 3 minutes. Empty bag into **CROCK-POT®** slow cooker. Gently toss beef and broccoli together. Serve over cooked rice. Garnish with sesame seeds, if desired.

Creamy Chicken and Spinach Lasagna

MAKES 4 SERVINGS | *PREP TIME:* 20 minutes
COOK TIME: LOW 3 hours

1¼ **cups shredded Swiss or mozzarella cheese, divided**

1 **cup ricotta cheese**

1 **teaspoon dried oregano**

¼ **teaspoon red pepper flakes**

1 **container (10 ounces) refrigerated Alfredo pasta sauce**

⅓ **cup water**

4 **no-boil lasagna noodles**

1 **package (10 ounces) frozen chopped spinach, thawed and squeezed dry**

¼ **cup grated Parmesan cheese**

1½ **cups cooked diced chicken**

Red pepper flakes, for garnish

1. Combine 1 cup cheese, ricotta, oregano and pepper flakes in small bowl; set aside. Blend Alfredo sauce with water; set aside.

2. Coat **CROCK-POT®** slow cooker with nonstick cooking spray. Break 2 lasagna noodles in half and place on bottom. Spread half of ricotta mixture over noodles. Top with half of spinach. Arrange half of chicken and half of Parmesan over spinach. Pour half of Alfredo mixture over top. Repeat layers, beginning with noodles and ending with Alfredo mixture. Cover; cook on LOW 3 hours.

3. Sprinkle remaining ¼ cup Swiss cheese on top. Cover and let stand 5 minutes or until cheese is melted. To serve, cut into squares or wedges. Garnish with pepper flakes, if desired.

Slow-Cooked Beef Brisket Dinner

MAKES 8 TO 10 SERVINGS

PREP TIME: 15 minutes
COOK TIME: LOW 6 to 8 hours

1 beef brisket (4 pounds), cut in half
4 to 6 medium potatoes, cut into large chunks
6 carrots, cut into 1-inch pieces
8 ounces mushrooms, sliced
½ large onion, sliced
1 stalk celery, cut into 1-inch pieces
3 cubes beef bouillon
5 cloves garlic, crushed
1 teaspoon black peppercorns
2 bay leaves
   Water, as needed
   Salt and black pepper, to taste
   Chopped parsley, for garnish

1. Place all ingredients in **CROCK-POT®** slow cooker. Add enough water to cover ingredients. Cover; cook on LOW 6 to 8 hours.

2. Remove and discard bay leaves. Transfer brisket to cutting board. Season with salt and pepper to taste. Slice meat across grain. Serve with vegetables. Garnish as desired.

Spicy Grits with Chicken

MAKES 6 SERVINGS | *PREP TIME:* 10 minutes
COOK TIME: LOW 4 hours

- **4 cups chicken broth**
- **1 cup grits***
- **1 jalapeño pepper,** cored, seeded and finely chopped**
- **½ teaspoon salt, or to taste**
- **¼ teaspoon paprika**
- **¼ teaspoon black pepper, or to taste**
- **¾ cup shredded sharp Cheddar cheese**
- **1½ cups chopped cooked chicken breast**
- **½ cup half-and-half**
- **2 tablespoons chopped chives, plus additional for garnish**

You may use coarse, instant, yellow or stone-ground grits.

**Jalapeño peppers can sting and irritate the skin, so wear rubber gloves when handling peppers and do not touch eyes.*

1. Combine broth, grits, jalapeño, salt, paprika and pepper in **CROCK-POT®** slow cooker. Stir well. Cover; cook on LOW 4 hours. (Consistency of cooked grits should be like cream of wheat.)

2. Add cheese and stir until melted. Stir in chicken, half-and-half and 2 tablespoons chives. Add salt and pepper, if desired. Cover; cook on LOW 15 minutes to blend flavors. Garnish with chives, if desired. Serve immediately.

No-Fuss Macaroni & Cheese

MAKES 6 TO 8 SERVINGS

PREP TIME: 10 minutes
COOK TIME: LOW 2 to 3 hours

2 cups (about 8 ounces) uncooked elbow macaroni
4 ounces light pasteurized processed cheese, cubed
1 cup (4 ounces) shredded mild Cheddar cheese
½ teaspoon salt
⅛ teaspoon black pepper
1½ cups fat-free (skim) milk

Combine macaroni, cheeses, salt and pepper in **CROCK-POT®** slow cooker. Pour milk over all. Cover; cook on LOW 2 to 3 hours, stirring after 20 to 30 minutes.

Baked Beans

MAKES 6 TO 8 SERVINGS

PREP TIME: 10 minutes
COOK TIME: LOW 8 to 12 hours
HIGH 3 to 4 hours

2 cans (16 ounces each) baked beans
1 cup ketchup
½ cup barbecue sauce
½ cup packed brown sugar
5 slices bacon, chopped
½ green bell pepper, chopped
½ onion, chopped
1½ teaspoons prepared mustard
Fresh parsley (optional)

Place all ingredients in **CROCK-POT®** slow cooker. Stir well to combine. Cover; cook on LOW 8 to 12 hours or on HIGH 3 to 4 hours. Garnish with fresh parsley, if desired.

Note: As with all macaroni and cheese dishes, the cheese sauce thickens and begins to dry as it sits. If the sauce dries, stir in a little extra milk and heat through. Do not cook longer than 4 hours.

No-Fuss
Macaroni & Cheese

Classic Pot Roast

MAKES 6 TO 8 SERVINGS

PREP TIME: 15 minutes
COOK TIME: LOW 8 to 10 hours

1 tablespoon vegetable oil
1 beef chuck shoulder roast (3 to 4 pounds)
6 medium potatoes, cut into halves
6 carrots, sliced
2 medium onions, cut into quarters
2 stalks celery, sliced
1 can (14½ ounces) diced tomatoes, undrained
   Salt and black pepper, to taste
   Dried oregano, to taste
   Water, as needed
1½ to 2 tablespoons all-purpose flour (optional)

1. Heat oil in large skillet over medium-low heat until hot. Add roast; brown on all sides. Drain and discard excess fat. Transfer roast to **CROCK-POT®** slow cooker.

2. Add potatoes, carrots, onions, celery and tomatoes with juice. Season with salt, pepper and oregano to taste. Add enough water to cover bottom of **CROCK-POT®** slow cooker by about ½ inch. Cover; cook on LOW 8 to 10 hours.

3. Transfer roast and vegetables to serving platter. To make gravy, whisk together cooking liquid and flour in small saucepan. Cook and stir over medium heat until thickened. Serve over roast and vegetables.

Meatballs and Spaghetti Sauce

MAKES 6 TO 8 SERVINGS

PREP TIME: 20 minutes
COOK TIME: LOW 3 to 5 hours
HIGH 2 to 4 hours

MEATBALLS

- 2 pounds 90% lean ground beef
- 1 cup bread crumbs
- 1 onion, chopped
- 2 eggs, beaten
- ¼ cup minced flat-leaf parsley
- 2 teaspoons minced garlic
- ½ teaspoon dry mustard
- ½ teaspoon black pepper
- Olive oil

SPAGHETTI SAUCE

- 1 can (28 ounces) peeled whole tomatoes, undrained
- ½ cup chopped fresh basil
- 2 tablespoons olive oil
- 2 garlic cloves, or to taste, finely minced
- 1 teaspoon sugar
- Salt and black pepper, to taste

- Cooked spaghetti
- Grated Parmesan cheese (optional)

1. Combine all meatball ingredients, except oil. Form into walnut-sized balls. Heat oil in skillet over medium heat until hot. Sear meatballs on all sides, turning as they brown. Transfer to **CROCK-POT®** slow cooker.

2. Combine all sauce ingredients in medium bowl. Pour over meatballs, stirring to coat. Cover; cook on LOW 3 to 5 hours or on HIGH 2 to 4 hours.

3. Adjust seasonings, if desired. Serve over spaghetti. Garnish with cheese, if desired.

Campfired-Up Sloppy Joes

MAKES 4 TO 6 SERVINGS

PREP TIME: 20 minutes
COOK TIME: HIGH 3 hours

1½ **pounds 90% lean ground beef**

½ **cup chopped sweet onion**

1 **medium red bell pepper, cored, seeded and chopped**

1 **large garlic clove, crushed**

½ **cup ketchup**

½ **cup barbecue sauce**

2 **tablespoons apple cider vinegar**

1 **tablespoon Worcestershire sauce**

1 **tablespoon packed brown sugar**

1 **teaspoon chili powder**

1 **can (8 ounces) baked beans**

6 **kaiser rolls, split and warmed**

Shredded sharp Cheddar cheese (optional)

1. Brown ground beef, onion, bell pepper and garlic 6 to 8 minutes in large skillet over medium-high heat, stirring to break up meat. Drain and discard excess fat. Transfer beef mixture to **CROCK-POT®** slow cooker.

2. Combine ketchup, barbecue sauce, vinegar, Worcestershire sauce, brown sugar and chili powder in small bowl. Transfer to **CROCK-POT®** slow cooker.

3. Add baked beans. Stir well to combine. Cover; cook on HIGH 3 hours.

4. To serve, fill split rolls with ½ cup sloppy joe mixture. Sprinkle with Cheddar cheese, if desired, before topping sandwich with roll lid.

Slow Cooker Chicken Dinner

MAKES 4 SERVINGS | *PREP TIME:* 5 minutes
COOK TIME: LOW 6 to 8 hours

4 boneless skinless chicken breasts

1 can (10¾ ounces) condensed cream of chicken soup, undiluted

⅓ cup milk

1 package (6 ounces) stuffing mix

1⅔ cups water

1. Place chicken in **CROCK-POT®** slow cooker. Combine soup and milk in small bowl; mix well. Pour soup mixture over chicken.

2. Combine stuffing mix and water. Spoon stuffing over chicken. Cover; cook on LOW 6 to 8 hours.

Favorite Chicken

MAKES 4 SERVINGS | *PREP TIME:* 15 minutes
COOK TIME: HIGH ½ hour plus LOW 6 to 8 hours

1 whole chicken (about 3 pounds), cut into pieces

1 cup chopped onion

1 cup sliced celery

1 cup sliced carrots

½ teaspoon seasoned salt

½ teaspoon black pepper

¼ teaspoon garlic powder

¼ teaspoon poultry seasoning

3 to 4 medium potatoes, cut into slices

1 can (14 ounces) chicken broth

Place chicken, onion, celery, carrots, seasoned salt, pepper, garlic powder and poultry seasoning in **CROCK-POT®** slow cooker. Top with potatoes. Add broth. Cover; cook on HIGH 30 minutes. Reduce heat to LOW. Cook on LOW 6 to 8 hours.

Slow Cooker Chicken Dinner

Chicken Noodle Soup

MAKES 4 SERVINGS

PREP TIME: 15 minutes

COOK TIME: LOW 5 to 7 hours,
HIGH 3 to 4 hours

1 can (48 ounces) chicken broth

2 boneless skinless chicken breasts, cut
     into bite-size pieces

4 cups water

⅔ cup diced onion

⅔ cup diced celery

⅔ cup diced carrots

⅔ cup sliced mushrooms

½ cup frozen peas

4 chicken bouillon cubes

2 tablespoons butter or margarine

1 tablespoon parsley flakes

1 teaspoon salt

1 teaspoon ground cumin

1 teaspoon dried marjoram

1 teaspoon black pepper

2 cups cooked egg noodles

Combine all ingredients except noodles in 5-quart
CROCK-POT® slow cooker. Cover; cook on LOW 5 to 7 hours
or on HIGH 3 to 4 hours. Add noodles 30 minutes before
serving.

Barbecued Pulled Pork Sandwiches

MAKES 8 SERVINGS

PREP TIME: 15 to 20 minutes
COOK TIME: LOW 12 to 14 hours
HIGH 6 to 7 hours

1 pork shoulder roast (about 2½ pounds)
1 bottle (14 ounces) barbecue sauce
1 tablespoon fresh lemon juice
1 teaspoon packed brown sugar
1 medium onion, chopped
8 hamburger buns or hard rolls

1. Place roast in **CROCK-POT®** slow cooker. Cover; cook on LOW 10 to 12 hours or on HIGH 5 to 6 hours.

2. Remove roast from **CROCK-POT®** slow cooker; discard cooking liquid. Shred pork using 2 forks. Return pork to **CROCK-POT®** slow cooker. Add barbecue sauce, lemon juice, brown sugar and onion. Cover; cook on LOW 2 hours or on HIGH 1 hour. Serve shredded pork on hamburger buns or hard rolls.

Tip: *For a 5, 6 or 7-quart* **CROCK-POT®** *slow cooker, double all ingredients, except for the barbecue sauce. Increase the barbecue sauce to 21 ounces.*

Super
SOUPS &
STEWS

BRING OUT THE BOWLS AND ENJOY
A HEARTY LUNCH OR DINNER

Irish Stew

MAKES 6 SERVINGS | *PREP TIME:* 15 minutes
| *COOK TIME:* LOW 7 to 9 hours

     1 cup fat-free reduced-sodium chicken broth
     1 teaspoon dried marjoram
     1 teaspoon dried parsley flakes
   ¾ teaspoon salt
   ½ teaspoon garlic powder
   ¼ teaspoon black pepper
1¼ pounds white potatoes, peeled and cut into 1-inch pieces
     1 pound lean lamb for stew, cut into 1-inch cubes
     8 ounces frozen cut green beans, thawed
     2 small leeks, cut lengthwise into halves,
         then crosswise into slices
1½ cups coarsely chopped carrots

1. Combine broth, marjoram, parsley, salt, garlic powder and pepper in large bowl; mix well. Transfer to **CROCK-POT®** slow cooker.

2. Layer potatoes, lamb, green beans, leeks and carrots into **CROCK-POT®** slow cooker. Cover; cook on LOW 7 to 9 hours or until lamb is tender.

Mexican Black Bean Bowl

MAKES 4 SERVINGS

PREP TIME: 10 minutes
COOK TIME: HIGH 3 to 4 hours

4 bone-in chicken thighs, skinned

1 cup finely chopped onion

1 can (14 ounces) fat-free chicken broth

1 can (14½ ounces) diced tomatoes with Mexican seasoning *or* diced tomatoes with green chilies, undrained

1 can (15 ounces) black beans, rinsed and drained

1 cup frozen corn

1 can (4 ounces) chopped mild green chilies

1 tablespoon chili powder

1 teaspoon ground cumin

1 teaspoon salt, or to taste

Optional toppings: sour cream, sliced avocado, shredded cheese, chopped cilantro, fried tortilla strips

1. Coat **CROCK-POT®** slow cooker with nonstick cooking spray. Add all ingredients, except toppings. Cover; cook on HIGH 3 to 4 hours or until chicken is done.

2. Remove chicken with slotted spoon. Debone and chop chicken. Return to **CROCK-POT®** slow cooker and stir well. Serve in bowls. Top as desired.

Note: *To skin chicken easily, grasp skin with paper towel and pull away. Repeat with fresh paper towel for each piece of chicken, discarding skins and towels.*

Creamy Farmhouse Chicken and Garden Soup

MAKES 4 SERVINGS

PREP TIME: 15 minutes
COOK TIME: HIGH 3 to 4 hours

- ½ package (16 ounces) frozen pepper stir-fry vegetable mix
- 1 cup frozen corn
- 1 medium zucchini, sliced
- 2 bone-in chicken thighs, skinned
- ½ teaspoon minced garlic
- 1 can (14 ounces) fat-free chicken broth
- ½ teaspoon dried thyme
- 2 ounces uncooked egg noodles
- 1 cup half-and-half
- ½ cup frozen green peas
- 2 tablespoons chopped parsley
- 2 tablespoons butter
- 1 teaspoon salt
- ½ teaspoon coarsely ground black pepper

1. Coat **CROCK-POT®** slow cooker with nonstick cooking spray. Place stir-fry vegetables, corn and zucchini in bottom. Add chicken, garlic, broth and thyme. Cover; cook on HIGH 3 to 4 hours or until chicken is no longer pink in center. Remove chicken and set aside to cool slightly.

2. Add noodles to **CROCK-POT®** slow cooker. Cover; cook 20 minutes longer, or until noodles are done.

3. Meanwhile, debone and chop chicken. Return to **CROCK-POT®** slow cooker. Stir in remaining ingredients. Let stand 5 minutes before serving.

Note: *To skin chicken easily, grasp skin with paper towel and pull away. Repeat with fresh paper towel for each piece of chicken, discarding skins and towels.*

Italian Sausage Soup

MAKES 4 TO 6 SERVINGS

PREP TIME: 15 minutes
COOK TIME: LOW 5 to 6 hours

SAUSAGE MEATBALLS

1 pound mild Italian sausage, casings removed
½ cup dried bread crumbs
¼ cup grated Parmesan cheese
¼ cup milk
1 egg
½ teaspoon dried basil
½ teaspoon black pepper
¼ teaspoon garlic salt

SOUP

4 cups hot chicken broth
1 tablespoon tomato paste
1 clove garlic, minced
¼ teaspoon red pepper flakes
½ cup mini pasta shells*
1 bag (10 ounces) baby spinach leaves
Shredded Parmesan cheese

Or use other tiny pasta, such as ditalini (mini tubes) or farfallini (mini bowties).

1. Combine all meatball ingredients. Form into marble-size balls.

2. Combine broth, tomato paste, garlic and red pepper flakes in **CROCK-POT®** slow cooker. Add meatballs. Cover; cook on LOW 5 to 6 hours.

3. Thirty minutes before serving, add pasta. When pasta is tender, stir in spinach leaves. Ladle into bowls, sprinkle with Parmesan cheese and serve immediately.

Curried Sweet Potato and Carrot Soup

MAKES 8 SERVINGS

PREP TIME: 10 minutes
COOK TIME: LOW 7 to 8 hours

2 medium-large sweet potatoes, peeled and cut into ¾-inch dice (about 5 cups)
2 cups baby carrots
1 small onion, chopped
¾ teaspoon curry powder
½ teaspoon salt, or to taste
½ teaspoon black pepper, or to taste
½ teaspoon ground cinnamon
¼ teaspoon ground ginger
4 cups chicken broth*
1 tablespoon maple syrup
¾ cup half-and-half
Candied ginger, for garnish

*If desired, add a teaspoon of chicken soup base along with the broth for richer flavor.

1. Place sweet potatoes, carrots, onion, curry powder, salt, pepper, cinnamon and ginger in 5-quart **CROCK-POT®** slow cooker. Add chicken broth. Stir well to combine. Cover; cook on LOW 7 to 8 hours.

2. Purée soup, 1 cup at a time, in blender. Return soup to **CROCK-POT®** slow cooker. (Or, use immersion blender.) Add maple syrup and half-and-half. Add salt and pepper, if desired. Cover; cook on HIGH 15 minutes to reheat. Serve in bowls and garnish with strips or pieces of candied ginger, if desired.

Sweet and Sour Brisket Stew

MAKES 6 TO 8 SERVINGS

PREP TIME: 10 minutes
COOK TIME: LOW 8 hours

1 jar (12 ounces) chili sauce

1½ to 2 tablespoons packed dark brown sugar

1½ tablespoons fresh lemon juice

¼ cup beef broth

1 tablespoon Dijon mustard

¼ teaspoon paprika

½ teaspoon salt, or to taste

¼ teaspoon black pepper, or to taste

1 garlic clove, minced

1 small onion, chopped

1 well-trimmed beef brisket, cut into 1-inch pieces*

2 large carrots, cut into ½-inch slices

1 tablespoon all-purpose flour (optional)

Beef brisket has a heavy layer of fat, which some supermarkets trim off. If the meat is trimmed, buy 2½ pounds; if not, purchase 4 pounds, then trim and discard excess fat.

1. Combine chili sauce, 1½ tablespoons brown sugar, lemon juice, broth, mustard, paprika, salt and pepper in 4- or 5-quart **CROCK-POT**® slow cooker. (Add remaining sugar, if desired, after tasting.)

2. Add garlic, onion, beef and carrots. Stir well to coat. Cover; cook on LOW 8 hours.

3. If thicker gravy is desired, combine 1 tablespoon flour and 3 tablespoons cooking liquid in small bowl. Add to **CROCK-POT**® slow cooker. Cover; cook on HIGH 10 minutes, or until thickened.

Smoked Sausage and Navy Bean Soup

MAKES 8 SERVINGS

PREP TIME: 15 minutes
COOK TIME: HIGH 8 to 9 hours

- 8 cups chicken broth
- 1 pound navy beans, rinsed
- 2 ham hocks (about 1 pound)
- 2 cloves garlic, minced
- 2 onions, diced
- 1 cup diced carrots
- 1 cup diced celery
- 1 can (14½ ounces) diced tomatoes, undrained
- 2 tablespoons tomato paste
- 1 bay leaf
- 1 teaspoon dried thyme
- 1 beef smoked sausage (16 ounces),
  cut into ½-inch rounds

1. Place broth in large saucepan. Heat over medium-high heat until broth begins to boil. Cover and reduce heat to low.

2. Place beans in 6-quart **CROCK-POT®** slow cooker. Add remaining ingredients, except broth and sausage. Carefully pour in hot broth. Cover; cook on HIGH 8 to 9 hours or until beans are tender.

3. Remove bay leaf. Remove ham hocks from **CROCK-POT®** slow cooker, and let stand until cool enough to handle. Remove ham from hocks, chop and add back to **CROCK-POT®** slow cooker. Stir in sausage. Cover; cook 15 to 30 minutes longer or until sausage is heated through.

Mushroom Barley Stew

MAKES 4 TO 6 SERVINGS | *PREP TIME:* 10 minutes
COOK TIME: LOW 6 to 7 hours

1 tablespoon olive oil
1 medium onion, finely chopped
1 cup chopped carrots (about 2 carrots)
1 clove garlic, minced
1 cup uncooked pearl barley
1 cup dried wild mushrooms, broken into pieces
1 teaspoon salt
½ teaspoon black pepper
½ teaspoon dried thyme
5 cups vegetable broth

1. Heat oil in medium skillet over medium-high heat until hot. Add onion, carrots and garlic. Cook and stir 5 minutes or until tender. Transfer to **CROCK-POT®** slow cooker.

2. Add barley, mushrooms, salt, pepper and thyme. Stir in broth. Cover; cook on LOW 6 to 7 hours. Adjust seasonings to taste.

Variation: *To turn this thick robust stew into a soup, add 2 to 3 cups of broth. Cook the same length of time.*

Chicken and Chile Pepper Stew

MAKES 6 SERVINGS

PREP TIME: 20 minutes
COOK TIME: LOW 8 to 9 hours

1 pound boneless skinless chicken thighs,
   cut into ½-inch pieces

1 pound small potatoes, cut lengthwise into halves,
   then crosswise into slices

1 cup chopped onion

2 poblano peppers,* seeded and
   cut into ½-inch pieces

1 jalapeño pepper,* seeded and finely chopped

3 cloves garlic, minced

3 cups fat-free reduced-sodium chicken broth

1 can (14 ounces) no-salt-added diced tomatoes,
   undrained

2 tablespoons chili powder

1 teaspoon dried oregano

Hot peppers can sting and irritate the skin, so wear rubber gloves when handling peppers and do not touch your eyes.

1. Place chicken, potatoes, onion, poblano peppers, jalapeño pepper and garlic in **CROCK-POT®** slow cooker.

2. Stir together broth, tomatoes with juice, chili powder and oregano in large bowl. Pour into **CROCK-POT®** slow cooker. Stir well to blend. Cover; cook on LOW 8 to 9 hours.

Hearty Lentil Stew

MAKES 6 SERVINGS

PREP TIME: 15 minutes
COOK TIME: LOW 9 to 11 hours

1 cup dried lentils, rinsed and sorted
1 package (16 ounces) frozen green beans, thawed
2 cups cauliflower florets
1 cup chopped onion
1 cup baby carrots, cut into halves crosswise
3 cups fat-free reduced-sodium chicken broth
2 teaspoons ground cumin
¾ teaspoon ground ginger
1 can (15 ounces) chunky tomato sauce
   with garlic and herbs
½ cup dry-roasted peanuts

1. Place lentils in **CROCK-POT®** slow cooker. Top with green beans, cauliflower, onion and carrots.

2. Combine broth, cumin and ginger in large bowl; mix well. Pour over vegetables in **CROCK-POT®** slow cooker. Cover; cook on LOW 9 to 11 hours.

3. Stir in tomato sauce. Cover; cook on LOW 10 minutes. Ladle stew into bowls. Sprinkle peanuts evenly over each serving.

Panama Pork Stew

MAKES 6 SERVINGS

PREP TIME: 15 minutes
COOK TIME: LOW 7 to 9 hours

2 small sweet potatoes (about ¾ pound), peeled and cut into 2-inch pieces
1 package (10 ounces) frozen corn
1 package (9 ounces) frozen cut green beans
1 cup chopped onion
1¼ pounds pork stew meat, cut into 1-inch cubes
1 can (14½ ounces) diced tomatoes, undrained
¼ cup water
1 to 2 tablespoons chili powder
½ teaspoon salt
½ teaspoon ground coriander

1. Place potatoes, corn, green beans and onion in **CROCK-POT®** slow cooker. Top with pork.

2. Combine tomatoes with juice, water, chili powder, salt and coriander in medium bowl. Pour over pork. Cover; cook on LOW 7 to 9 hours.

Easy
ENTERTAINING

SPEND MORE TIME WITH GUESTS WHILE YOUR CROCK-POT® SLOW COOKER DOES THE WORK

Cherry Rice Pudding

MAKES 6 SERVINGS

PREP TIME: 10 minutes
COOK TIME: LOW 4 to 5 hours

1½ **cups milk**
1 **cup hot cooked rice**
3 **eggs, beaten**
½ **cup sugar**
¼ **cup dried cherries or cranberries**
½ **teaspoon almond extract**
¼ **teaspoon salt**
Ground nutmeg, for garnish

1. Combine all ingredients in large bowl. Pour into greased 1½-quart casserole dish. Cover dish with buttered aluminum foil, butter side down.

2. Place rack in 5-quart **CROCK-POT®** slow cooker and pour in 1 cup water. Place casserole on rack. Cover; cook on LOW 4 to 5 hours.

3. Remove casserole from **CROCK-POT®** slow cooker. Let stand 15 minutes before serving. Garnish with nutmeg, if desired.

Pepperoni Pizza Dip with Breadstick Dippers

MAKES 8 SERVINGS

PREP TIME: 20 minutes
COOK TIME: LOW 2 hours
HIGH 1 to 1½ hours

1 jar or can (14 ounces) pizza sauce
¾ cup chopped turkey pepperoni
4 green onions, chopped
1 can (2¼ ounces) sliced black olives, drained
½ teaspoon dried oregano
1 cup (4 ounces) shredded mozzarella cheese
1 package (3 ounces) cream cheese, softened
Breadstick Dippers (recipe follows)

1. Combine pizza sauce, pepperoni, green onions, olives and oregano in 2-quart **CROCK-POT®** slow cooker. Cover; cook on LOW 2 hours or on HIGH 1 to 1½ hours or until mixture is hot.

2. Stir in mozzarella and cream cheese until melted and well blended. Serve with warm breadsticks.

Breadstick Dippers

1 package (8 ounces) refrigerated breadstick dough
2 teaspoons melted butter
2 teaspoons minced parsley

Bake breadsticks according to package directions. Brush with melted butter and sprinkle with parsley. Serve with warm dip.

Shrimp Louisiana-Style

MAKES 3 TO 4 SERVINGS

PREP TIME: 5 minutes

COOK TIME: HIGH 1¼ hours

  1 **pound shrimp, unpeeled, rinsed**
½ **cup (1 stick) butter, diced**
⅓ **cup lemon juice**
  1 **tablespoon Worcestershire sauce**
  1 **teaspoon minced garlic**
  1 **teaspoon seafood seasoning**
½ **teaspoon salt**
½ **teaspoon coarsely ground black pepper**
1½ **teaspoons grated lemon peel, plus additional for garnish**
    Hot cooked rice (optional)
  4 **lemon wedges (optional)**

1. Coat **CROCK-POT**® slow cooker with nonstick cooking spray. Place shrimp in bottom. Add butter, lemon juice, Worcestershire sauce, garlic, seafood seasoning, salt and pepper. Stir well to combine. Cover; cook on HIGH 1¼ hours.

2. Turn off **CROCK-POT**® slow cooker. Stir in 1½ teaspoons lemon peel. Let stand, uncovered, 5 minutes. Serve in shallow soup bowl over rice, if desired. Garnish with grated lemon peel and serve with lemon wedge, if desired.

Hot Tropics Sipper

MAKES 8 SERVINGS

PREP TIME: 5 minutes
COOK TIME: HIGH 3½ to 4 hours

4 cups pineapple juice

2 cups apple juice

1 container (11.3 ounces) apricot nectar

3 whole cinnamon sticks

6 whole cloves

½ cup packed dark brown sugar

1 medium lemon, thinly sliced

1 medium orange, thinly sliced

Additional lemon and orange slices, for garnish

Place all ingredients in **CROCK-POT®** slow cooker. Cover; cook on HIGH 3½ to 4 hours, or until very fragrant. Strain immediately (beverage will turn bitter if fruit and spices remain after cooking is complete). Serve with fresh slices of orange and lemon, if desired.

Spicy Sweet & Sour Cocktail Franks

MAKES ABOUT 4 DOZEN | *PREP TIME:* 5 minutes
COOK TIME: LOW 2 to 3 hours

2 packages (8 ounces each) cocktail franks
½ cup ketchup or chili sauce
½ cup apricot preserves
1 teaspoon hot pepper sauce
Additional hot pepper sauce (optional)

1. Combine all ingredients in 1½-quart **CROCK-POT®** slow cooker; mix well. Cover; cook on LOW 2 to 3 hours.

2. Serve warm or at room temperature with additional hot pepper sauce, if desired.

Angel Wings

MAKES 2 SERVINGS | *PREP TIME:* 5 minutes
COOK TIME: LOW 5 to 6 hours

1 can (10¾ ounces) condensed tomato soup, undiluted
¾ cup water
¼ cup packed light brown sugar
2½ tablespoons balsamic vinegar
2 tablespoons chopped shallots
10 chicken wings

1. Combine soup, water, brown sugar, vinegar and shallots in **CROCK-POT®** slow cooker; mix well.

2. Add chicken wings; stir to coat with sauce. Cover; cook on LOW 5 to 6 hours or until cooked through and glazed with sauce.

Spicy Sweet & Sour
Cocktail Franks

Chicken Cordon Bleu

MAKES 4 SERVINGS

PREP TIME: 20 minutes
COOK TIME: LOW 2 hours

- ¼ **cup all-purpose flour**
- 1 **teaspoon paprika**
- ½ **teaspoon salt**
- ¼ **teaspoon black pepper**
- 4 **boneless chicken breasts, lightly pounded***
- 4 **slices ham**
- 4 **slices Swiss cheese**
- 2 **tablespoons olive oil**
- ½ **cup white cooking wine**
- ½ **cup chicken broth**
- ½ **cup half-and-half**
- 2 **tablespoons cornstarch**

Place chicken between 2 pieces of plastic food wrap and flatten with back of skillet.

1. Combine flour, paprika, salt and pepper in resealable plastic food storage bag and shake well; set aside.

2. Place flattened chicken on cutting board, skin side down. Place 1 slice ham and 1 slice cheese on each piece. Fold chicken up to enclose filling, and secure with toothpick. Place in bag with seasoned flour, and shake gently to coat.

3. Heat oil in large skillet over medium-high heat until hot. Add chicken, skin side down. Brown on all sides. Transfer to **CROCK-POT®** slow cooker.

4. Remove skillet from heat and add wine. Cook and stir to loosen browned bits. Pour into **CROCK-POT®** slow cooker. Add broth. Cover; cook on LOW 2 hours.

5. Remove chicken with slotted spoon. Cover with aluminum foil to keep warm. Mix together half-and-half and cornstarch. Add to cooking liquid. Cover, cook 15 minutes longer or until sauce has thickened. To serve, remove toothpicks, place chicken on plates and spoon sauce around chicken. Serve extra sauce on side.

Asian Barbecue Skewers

MAKES 4 TO 6 SERVINGS | *PREP TIME:* 10 minutes
COOK TIME: LOW 3 hours

2 pounds boneless skinless chicken thighs
½ cup soy sauce
⅓ cup packed brown sugar
2 tablespoons sesame oil
3 cloves garlic, minced
½ cup thinly sliced scallions
1 tablespoon toasted sesame seeds (optional)

1. Cut each thigh into 4 pieces about 1½ inches thick. Thread chicken onto 7-inch-long wooden skewers, folding thinner pieces, if necessary. Place skewers into 6-quart **CROCK-POT®** slow cooker, layering as flat as possible.

2. Combine soy sauce, brown sugar, oil and garlic in small bowl. Reserve ⅓ cup sauce; set aside. Pour remaining sauce over skewers. Cover; cook on LOW 2 hours. Turn skewers over and cook 1 hour longer.

3. Transfer skewers to serving platter. Discard cooking liquid. Spoon on reserved sauce and sprinkle with sliced scallions and sesame seeds, if desired.

Chocolate Hazelnut Pudding Cake

MAKES 10 SERVINGS

PREP TIME: 5 minutes
COOK TIME: HIGH 2½ hours

1 box (18¼ ounces) golden yellow cake mix
1 cup water
4 eggs
½ cup sour cream
½ cup vegetable oil
1 cup semisweet chocolate mini morsels
½ cup chopped hazelnuts
Whipped cream or ice cream (optional)

1. Coat 6-quart **CROCK-POT®** slow cooker with nonstick cooking spray. Combine cake mix, water, eggs, sour cream and oil; mix smooth. Pour batter into **CROCK-POT®** slow cooker. Cover; cook on HIGH 2 hours, or until batter is nearly set.

2. Sprinkle on mini morsels and hazelnuts. Cover; cook 30 minutes longer, or until toothpick inserted into center comes out clean or cake begins to pull away from sides of **CROCK-POT®** slow cooker. Let stand until cool and slice, or spoon out while warm. Serve with whipped cream, if desired.

Turkey Breast with Sweet Cranberry-Soy Sauce

MAKES 8 SERVINGS

PREP TIME:	10 minutes
COOK TIME:	HIGH 3½ hours

- 1 bone-in turkey breast, thawed, rinsed and patted dry (6 to 7 pounds)*
- 1 can (16 ounces) whole berry cranberry sauce
- 1 packet (1 ounce) dry onion soup mix
- Grated peel and juice of 1 medium orange
- 3 tablespoons soy sauce
- 2 to 3 tablespoons cornstarch
- 1 to 1½ tablespoons sugar
- 1 to 1½ teaspoons cider vinegar
- Salt, to taste

You may substitute 2 (3½-pound) bone-in turkey breast halves, if necessary.

1. Coat 6- or 7-quart **CROCK-POT®** slow cooker with nonstick cooking spray. Place turkey in bottom, meat side up. Combine cranberry sauce, soup mix, orange peel and orange juice in small bowl. Pour over turkey. Cover; cook on HIGH 3½ hours.

2. Scrape cranberry mixture into cooking liquid. Transfer turkey to cutting board. Let stand 15 minutes before slicing.

3. Combine soy sauce and cornstarch in small bowl. Stir into cooking liquid with sugar, vinegar and salt, if desired. Cover; cook on HIGH 15 minutes longer, or until thickened slightly. Serve sauce over sliced turkey.

Artichoke and Nacho Cheese Dip

MAKES ABOUT 1 QUART

PREP TIME: 5 minutes
COOK TIME: LOW 2 hours

- 2 cans (10¾ ounces each) condensed nacho cheese soup
- 1 can (14 ounces) quartered artichoke hearts, drained and coarsely chopped
- 1 cup (4 ounces) shredded or thinly sliced pepper jack cheese
- 1 can (4 ounces) evaporated milk
- 2 tablespoons minced chives, divided
- ½ teaspoon paprika
  Crackers or chips

1. Combine soup, artichoke hearts, cheese, milk, 1 tablespoon chives and paprika in **CROCK-POT®** slow cooker. Cover; cook on LOW 2 hours.

2. Stir well. Sprinkle with remaining 1 tablespoon chives and serve with crackers.

Apple Crumble Pot

MAKES 6 TO 8 SERVINGS

PREP TIME: 15 minutes
COOK TIME: HIGH 2¼ hours

FILLING

⅔ **cup packed dark brown sugar**

2 **tablespoons prepared baking mix**

1½ **teaspoons ground cinnamon**

¼ **teaspoon ground allspice**

½ **cup dried cranberries**

2 **tablespoons butter, cubed**

1 **teaspoon vanilla**

4 **Granny Smith apples, cored and cut into 8 wedges each (about 2 pounds)**

TOPPING

1 **cup prepared baking mix**

½ **cup rolled oats**

⅓ **cup packed dark brown sugar**

3 **tablespoons cold butter, cubed**

½ **cup chopped pecans**

1. Prepare filling: Coat **CROCK-POT®** slow cooker with nonstick cooking spray. Combine brown sugar, baking mix, cinnamon and allspice in large bowl. Add remaining filling ingredients, and toss gently to coat evenly. Transfer to **CROCK-POT®** slow cooker.

2. Prepare topping: Combine baking mix, oats and brown sugar in same large bowl. Cut in butter with pastry blender or 2 knives until mixture resembles pea-sized crumbs. Sprinkle evenly over filling in **CROCK-POT®** slow cooker. Top with pecans. Cover; cook on HIGH 2¼ hours or until apples are tender. *Do not overcook.*

3. Turn off **CROCK-POT®** slow cooker. Uncover, and let stand 15 to 30 minutes before serving. Garnish as desired.

Turkey with Pecan-Cherry Stuffing

MAKES 8 SERVINGS

PREP TIME: 20 minutes
COOK TIME: LOW 5 to 6 hours

1 fresh or frozen boneless turkey breast (about 3 to 4 pounds)
2 cups cooked rice
⅓ cup chopped pecans
⅓ cup dried cherries or cranberries
1 teaspoon poultry seasoning
¼ cup peach, apricot or plum preserves
1 teaspoon Worcestershire sauce

1. Thaw turkey breast, if frozen. Remove skin and discard. Cut slices three-fourths of the way through turkey at 1-inch intervals.

2. Stir together rice, pecans, cherries and poultry seasoning in large bowl. Stuff rice mixture between slices. If necessary, skewer turkey lengthwise to hold it together. Transfer to **CROCK-POT®** slow cooker.

3. Cover; cook on LOW 5 to 6 hours or until turkey registers 170°F on meat thermometer inserted into thickest part of breast, not touching stuffing.

4. Stir together preserves and Worcestershire sauce. Spoon over turkey. Cover; let stand for 5 minutes. Remove skewer before serving.

Spicy Orange Chicken Nuggets

MAKES ABOUT 54 NUGGETS

PREP TIME: 15 minutes
COOK TIME: LOW 3 to 3½ hours

- 1 bag (28 ounces) frozen popcorn chicken bites
- 1½ cups prepared honey teriyaki marinade
- ¾ cup orange juice concentrate
- ⅔ cup water
- 1 tablespoon orange marmalade
- ¾ teaspoon hot chile sauce *or* sriracha*
- Thinly sliced scallions, for garnish
- Hot cooked rice

Sriracha is a Thai hot sauce, also called "rooster sauce" because of the label on the bottle, and is available in Asian specialty markets.

1. Preheat oven to 450°F. Spread chicken evenly on baking sheet. Bake 12 to 14 minutes or until crisp. (Do not brown.) Transfer to **CROCK-POT®** slow cooker.

2. Combine teriyaki marinade, juice concentrate, water, marmalade and chile sauce in medium bowl. Pour over chicken. Cover; cook on LOW 3 to 3½ hours.

3. Sprinkle with scallions and serve with rice.

INDEX